A Year in the Woods:
Reflections on Leading an
Outdoor Parent-and-Child Group

Margaret Madeline Loescher

WECAN
WALDORF EARLY CHILDHOOD
ASSOCIATION OF NORTH AMERICA

Text and photography: Margaret Loescher
Copy Editing: Lory Widmer
Graphic Design: Sheila Harrington, Studio Five

This publication was made possible by a grant from the Waldorf Curriculum Fund.

© Margaret Loescher, 2015
First English Edition

Cover photograph: Cedar exploring the bird bath
Opposite: Whitsun dove wreath

"The Tree Song" adapted and reprinted by kind permission
of Lorraine Lee Hammond.
© 1979, Lorraine Lee Hammond, Snowy Egret Music, BMI.

"Wake Up," "Here's a Branch of Snowy May," and "Busy Bee" reprinted from
The Singing Year by Candy Verney, by kind permission of Hawthorn Press
(www.hawthornpress.com).
© 2006 Candy Verney

Published in the United States
by the Waldorf Early Childhood Association of North America
285 Hungry Hollow Road
Spring Valley, NY 10977
845-352-1690
info@waldorfearlychildhood.org
www.waldorfearlychildhood.org

ISBN: 978-1-936849-31-4

*For the children
of Heartwood,
past, present
and future.*

**In memory of
Emily Kate Evison**

Acknowledgements

I would like to thank Jane and Nick Wise for their generosity
in sharing with us their beautiful woods,
Jenny Davey for believing in me,
Joel and Cedar Chalfen for behind the scenes support,
especially packing the bike every Tuesday morning,
and all the families of Heartwood for bringing with them
a kindred spirit no matter the weather.
I wish to thank Managing Editor Lory Widmer,
graphic designer Sheila Harrington,
and the staff at WECAN for their commitment
to making my words and photographs into a book.

Contents

Foreword

Heartwood embodies a few of the secrets of those things that draw us together.

Left: Onyx and Archie rolling out the fire bread dough

Parent-and-child groups have arisen over the past decades in a variety of forms. We have a deep desire to form groups, to come together, to find a place for our children and for ourselves, hoping to find meaning and feel settled. In Waldorf education these groups are taking on ever-varied forms, some indoors with the form and rhythm of home, some with a focus on deepening our understanding of child development, all with the simple and brave hope of creating a safe place for children and families to gather together. Each form, filled with good intentions, will offer gifts to the children and families who attend.

Margaret Madeline Loescher found Heartwood out of her own need for a like-minded community in which to parent her child. It grew into a true community, a place that gave generously to those who gathered there. The program was crafted out of her deep sense of the needs of the young child, of the child's world, as she refers to it. She resisted the temptation to do things in an "adult way" and left the child as the center. The earnest desire to meet those parents who come toward us informs all of us who work with parents and children. In doing so we sometimes lose the child at the center, but Margaret's book so clearly shows that if you create a program that nourishes children, it will nourish adults in turn. We all crave rhythm and predictability. We all long to make beautiful things from simple materials with our own hands. We all long to know a place in its varied seasons, on the dark days and in the light.

Margaret chose to make her home for children and their families in the forest. She instinctively knew that the group would be well supported by nature in Her kindness. She found a well-loved wood with a special history of being privately owned but open and welcoming to others, a special place for many people of all ages. Here the families could witness change, become part of a place, know and be known by it. She wisely crafted a solid rhythm that shifted as the seasons shifted, but had a strong enough form to offer comfort and certainty, and she knew that simplicity offers depth. And then she celebrated. *A Year in the Woods* is full of rhyme and song. There are crafts and verses for each season of the year, inspiring teachers and parents alike to find a place and make it their own and rejoice. Nature offers herself to us with such generosity and kindness, and she loves to have us celebrate her in turn.

Heartwood embodies a few of the secrets of those things that draw us together; fire, food, friendship, constancy, a sense of place, something well-prepared, an offering made with love. Margaret beautifully shares her gifts with us, inspiring us to make meaning and nourish one another. She astutely leaves enough space for the child to celebrate the world in which he is so new.

Magdalena Toran
October, 2015

Magdalena Toran is a parent-and-child teacher at The Hartsbrook School in Hadley, Massachusetts. She feels deeply grateful for the work of welcoming families as they find their way into creating and sustaining a nourishing life. She has been a member of the WECAN Board since 2014.

Jay, Joel and Onyx
cooking the fire bread

Prologue:
Finding Heartwood

*I*n August, 2010, a year before this story begins, my husband Joel and I, together with our daughter, Cedar, had moved to Lincoln, a city in the east midlands in England. We knew no one in our new town. Cedar was about to turn one, and Joel was starting a new, very demanding job. Previously, I had been a writer, and I had plans to look after Cedar and fit writing in around mothering duties—a plan that I knew would take a great deal of energy and enthusiasm. Unfortunately, I found neither in the first few months of living in Lincoln. I began searching for a playgroup I liked in the hopes that I would find like-minded parents and perhaps a community. But local groups made me feel even worse. Very little of consequence seemed to pass between parents and between children. Outdoor spaces, if there were any, were covered in concrete, and the children were offered sugary snacks and drinks. I began to wonder if this was our lot.

Then Joel, Cedar and I met Jay and his son Archie at a community cafe. Jay had an air of challenge and revolution about him. His son Archie had fiery red hair and a certain energy that I liked. Jay told us about a new group, just started, that met in some nearby woods. We went the following week, and after our first attendance rescheduled our week to make sure we could always attend. And so began much-needed relationships with people and a place that would see us through gloomier times and into a whole new way of thinking about children, about parenthood, and about the outdoors.

Left: Cedar exploring the bird bath

Introduction

Any successful parent-and-child group is about the whole group of attendees.

Left: Self-portrait in the broken mirrors in the roots of a tree

*I*n August, 2011, almost a year after Cedar and I began attending the Lincolnshire Parent and Child Woods Group, I volunteered as the new leader, a position I held for a year until we left Lincoln. During this time I kept a diary of our meetings in the woods and occasionally took photographs.

One may rightfully argue that playing in the woods and an early childhood setting that is informed by Waldorf education both fall within the domain of "doing" and "being," and so one may ask, why write and take photographs? My answer is two-fold. First and foremost, I cannot help it! I am, by trade a writer and an image-maker. I have always had a need to record events and archive them.

Secondly, over the course of my year in the woods, I developed a burning necessity to pass on what I learned. I saw a need for a book that told stories about leading a parent-and-child group and offered resources to future outdoor group leaders and parents. Such a book would offer not just the words of seasonal songs or craft ideas, but my doubts, my successes and failures, my constant learning process, and my love of a very special outdoor space.

Any successful parent-and-child group is about the whole group of attendees. They, too, have experienced a year in the woods and they too have their own record of events, in the memories they

1

may have formed, in the crafted objects they may have kept, and certainly in the friendships they have built; in the experiences of the trees, the moss, the nettles, as they change throughout the year; and in the witnessing of each other, adult and child alike as they, too, grow. I offer the following pages as my own witnessing and learning with deep appreciation and acknowledgment of theirs, too.

Heartwood

Near an established village about six miles outside of the city of Lincoln lies a patch of woodland divided into several plots. One of these plots has been owned by Jane and Nick for many years. By law, they are not able to build on it. They have erected a few temporary structures to allow shelter from extreme weather conditions. They manage their eight acres of woodland themselves and they often host gatherings to celebrate winter and summer solstices, seasonal festivities, birthdays, singing and craft parties. The Lincolnshire Parent and Child Group was first invited to use it in the autumn of 2010.

Heartwood is a mixture of beech, chestnut, and oak with some fruit trees (mostly cherry and plum) left over from a bygone era when the land was probably used as an orchard. The beech trees are the most impressive to me. They are very tall, and demand space, so that they create under their canopy a certain atmosphere that is quintessentially woods.

We looked after each other in Heartwood for it was, after all, a wild place.

Our parent-and-child group was a bit noisy for the spotting of wildlife but we did find plenty of ladybugs and other insects when the season was right. A neighbor's plot adjacent to Jane's has a clearing in which he keeps bees, and on occasion we walked within safe distance to have a look. We spotted rabbits and grey squirrels, and once rescued two baby hedgehogs. Jane has seen a deer.

These are well-loved woods. One can tell that immediately by the way the space has been arranged and adorned with woodland-inspired

Jane, Robin and Archie at song time

decorations. There is a central focus in a clearing near the entrance. A fallen beech creates a natural edge to this clearing, in the center of which is the fire pit, an ash-covered spot encircled with broken bricks and stones. When our group met we added our willow-weave fireguard to keep the children about three feet away from the fire. On two of the other sides of this focal area are tent-like structures made from parts of trees, willow branches, and canvas. Inside them are pieces of garden furniture. Next to one of these tents is something between a mantelpiece and an altar or offering table: a cross-section of a tree balances like a table top on the top of a sawn off trunk. Candles are often placed here, and interesting objects that have been found in the woods: small skulls, feathers, stones.

There are many paths that cut through the thicker undergrowth and a main path that runs around the entire woodland, loosely following the boundary line. Along these paths there are often objects of great interest, either naturally occurring (the tree with the low canopy that is wonderful to hide under, the fallen tree with the pit of exposed roots that is enticing to dig at) or man-made, placed there by someone in a creative spirit (a wicker structure that looks like a big witch's hat hanging in a tree, a rusty bicycle leaning up against another, the face of a man carved into wood, a labyrinth made from stones). There is also a composting toilet, a tire swing on a very tall beech, and a small hill made from sandy earth, commonly referred to as a "ship" by the children. There is a willow dome built by one of our parents, and a woodland stage, a wooden platform supported by three trees and raised off the ground by a few feet.

The families that feature in these pages often made long journeys to Heartwood once a week, coming from Lincoln and from the surrounding villages. Some families drove from far away, often sharing lifts with one another. Some took the bus from Lincoln, being dropped in the village and walking across the fields and into the woods. Cedar and I cycled in our Dutch cargo bike, past a factory, along a canal and through a chain of villages and into the countryside. These journeys were important. They defined Heartwood as a special place, a place outside of our daily lives, a place far away and in a different realm. I think it is partly as a result of these weekly journeys to the woods that the group became very close and family-like during the course of the two years that it ran. We looked after each other in Heartwood, for it was, after all, a wild place.

Seasons and Rhythms

Outdoors we are working with the ever-changing seasonal rhythms. It cannot be denied that winter has a very different rhythm from summer, for instance. In a playgroup, how do we respect this and yet form a continuity that can hold the children and give them a sense of security in this big, wild place in every season? Little children need solidity, certainty, clarity. And yet, here were the woods, so different each time! And not just in the temperature, the humidity, the color of the sky or earth or leaf, but in the temperament, the mood, the spirit. And so in the rhythm that we followed we attempted to bring certainty to uncertainty: we built fires in the rain, ate picnics in the snow, simply because we always built a fire, we always had a picnic. The running order of events during the group was always the same. This was as follows:

Arrival

Welcome tea for adults and a little snack for children

(for example, a piece of apple, a small rice cake)

Craft activity and free play

Circle time (the singing of songs)

Lunch

Woods wander

Story

Parting song

In keeping to a rhythm it was also important to me to respect seasonal changes and the needs of the children in relation to them. The length of each activity sometimes altered due to weather and level of interest. For instance if it was cold the craft activity might not last so long, as hands got cold working with small bits of leaves, wire, or clay. Fire building and maintenance took up much more time in the winter, and the lunch tended to be needed a little earlier, with a warm food included such as baked potatoes. In the winter we spent more time near the fire, eating there. In the warmer weather we ate in the willow dome. The woods wander tended to be longer in the warmer months when the woods were denser and there was more to explore visually as well as physically.

I learned that it was important when making these changes to do so with a strong sense of regularity and certainty. There was nothing more unsettling for the children and for the adults than an active discussion or debate during the running of the group as to what would happen next and where it would happen. So changes were rarely made on a daily basis, but instead on a seasonal basis. We would keep to the summer eating place or wandering route when it was summer and shift only when the season changed.

From a settled rhythm grew an ability to find comfort and certainty in all the seasonal changes around us, and an underlying knowledge of their cyclical nature.

Being in the Children's World

Sustenance

Over time, I learned that the length of the journeys made by many of our attendees meant that the children arrived hungry and spent much of the morning asking when lunch would be. Because of this I introduced a small welcome snack to settle stomachs and nerves. Lunch, to which everyone contributed, became a little bit too elaborate for my liking, but suggested a need of the children and adults for sustenance in the woods.

Woodland Wander

I soon became aware that taking a proper walk through the woods was not appropriate for children so young and so we did not walk in a linear fashion so much as explore. I tried to follow the children's interests and be in their world when wandering in the woods. To set a destination more suitable for adults was always tempting and had to be resisted.

Storytelling

Storytelling was very important in establishing a rhythm and in mirroring back to the children their experiences in the woods. Jane, who led the group before me, began the group with an active story, one that incorporated circle time and that had the participating families stand up and act out parts of the story. I had heard about this being done in other outdoor groups. An active story made much sense from the perspective of keeping warm. For various reasons I chose to bring the story down to the ground and tell it as a puppet show with felt figures, pieces of material, and found objects from the woods. I also changed the time that the story was told, moving it to the close of the group in order for it to reflect some of the events that had happened to the children and in the woods that very morning. The story, therefore, became a way in which the children could relate to their own experiences.

I was conscious of working within some Waldorf story-telling guidelines. It is important, when telling stories to children under three (of

What is the relative nature of beauty for those to whom the world is so new?

which we had a number) to have some constants, often in the form of regular and recognizable characters that appear in every story. It is also important not to have too much fantasy in the story, as very young children are still learning about the real world and need to see real role models with realistic interactions. For instance, animals should not speak or wear clothes or be in any other way personified. Fairies, gnomes, and other fantasy creatures are more appropriate for children over three. Stories should be positive without scary or dark encounters and they should, in some way, represent the life and interests of children.

I sewed two felt figures, a boy and a girl with stocky, tubular bodies and no arms or legs. Peter had a belt, which was good for tucking small feathers into, and a collar. Lilly had curly hair. They both had round heads that bobbed slightly when the figures were moved and no facial features. They were stuffed well but not too tightly so that with a certain squeeze of the hand holding their bodies, they could bow or turn their heads upwards to look at the trees or the sky. Peter and Lilly featured in all of the stories I told in the woods and their adventures often reflected the adventures the children had gone on during the course of the morning. They began with them waking up and leaving the house, and they closed with them returning from the woods and going to bed.

A couple of months after I took on the role of leader, I introduced a river and a felt swan into the story, bought from a woman in a yurt in Mongolia years before. In their journey to the woods Peter and Lilly crossed the river, either over a bridge or, in warmer months, taking off their shoes and wading across. Sometimes they had a rowboat. In the crossing of the river they met the swan. She never spoke and seldom created the focus of the plot, but she was always present. Peter and Lilly would bow to the swan, crossing the river as they did so, and the swan, it seemed to them, would bow in return. Without my really thinking about it, the swan became a symbol of the majesty of the woods and the respect which we carried in

Picnic time in the willow dome

order to be here and in each other's company. So, too, had the river become a symbol. There is no body of water in Heartwood, so its presence in the story did not reflect our real environment. The river was useful as a symbol of a boundary, like the boundaries that we all crossed when we came away from the comforts of our own lives into the woods to meet one another, to communicate, and to explore.

In a workshop with Deb Wilenski at Steiner House in London, I learned about the success of allowing the children to bring found objects to contribute to the story. In this way the children's interest in the telling of the story was heightened and it ensured that the story reflected the setting. This device also kept the storyteller on her toes and the story fresh and full of imagination, as one never knew what objects would be placed down to be incorporated at story time. In Heartwood the children immediately embraced the idea of collecting things for the story. I was showered with sticks, short and long and in-between, with funny knobs and smooth sides; moss in clumps; leaves, silky, rough, gnarled, spotted, this year's and last year's; bark, mold, insects, rubbish, feathers and stones. And as I watched the children collect these wonders, I remembered a mother once said that on suggesting the children in her care find "a beautiful leaf," she realized that to them all leaves are beautiful. For what is the relative nature of beauty for those to whom the world is so new?

Autumn: Copper Leaves and Fantastic Thighs

When we arrived for our time in the woods, they, too, held possibility.

Left: Evan and Atticus

September

September is an extra month. Summer is definitely over, one cannot deny that. Autumn is dawning, but the onslaught of winter has not yet been accepted. In the meantime there is September, the month of harvest. I have always found it a month of possibility. Cedar was born in September, on the day before Michaelmas. When we arrived for our time in the woods, they, too, held possibility. The horse chestnuts had begun to fall and push their smooth heads from the unfriendly bristles in which they grew. Half-open eyes, looking at us from amongst the leaves. . . treasures of seeing.

We pulled into the bumpy parking place and found the wheelbarrow already usefully and unexpectedly leaning up against the nearest tree. Cedar, as usual, wanted to ride in it. Sue and Elise pulled up and helped us load the equipment into it instead—cold water for washing hands, several small squares cut from old dish towels, soap in a dish, baked potatoes, still hot, wrapped and in a box, rice cakes and cut-up fruit for the children as a small welcome snack, a thermos of boiled water for tea, a selection of tea bags and cups for the parents when they arrived, a large tarpaulin, a picnic blanket. There was a basket full of the story-telling things: Peter and Lilly and the felt swan, green material for the grass, white wool for the sky, and a blue bandana for the river. We had matches, newspaper, kindling, and the craft materials, which today included a mammoth green summer squash to create into our Michaelmas dragon. And Cedar's potty balanced on top of it all.

I liked arriving at the woods early so that I could be ready to greet everyone as they came. Onyx, who was the eldest child in the group, had run ahead of his mother, Jenny G. He slowed down as he approached and took a moment to be shy, noticing who else was present. Archie would often launch into a conversation directly—something he was talking about on his journey on the bus, or something he had for breakfast. Elise asked about the snack. Oscar and Kai were quiet and kept close to their respective mothers, Jenny D. and Paula. Occasionally Jane, the owner of Heartwood, would attend with her

Onyx, Archie and Jenny G. "cooking" leaves and sticks

> **The older boys were particularly enthusiastic fire builders.**

granddaughter, Robin. Jane always brought much warmth and enthusiasm and lovely songs. Robin was shy. Evan was often very enthusiastic when he arrived. He seemed to relish the first encounter, always being ahead of his mother, Jaime, and appearing from behind the shelter, grinning, as if we were all sharing a miraculous secret which we had been patiently containing and were just now announcing to the world. Sometimes he would exclaim, throwing his arms wide in the air; Atticus, cooler, by his side. This morning Evan and Atticus got busy straight away, using large sticks to push leaves into piles.

I handed out the crowns we had been making the previous week. Jay, Archie's father, built a blazing fire. I often marveled at the way in which he took such care and creative spirit in building something that would moments later go up in smoke. The older boys were particularly enthusiastic fire builders and they kept bringing large logs from the log pile. On each trip to the log pile they spent a little more time in the log pile and a little less time actually transporting the logs to the fire place, until the game seemed to be entirely based in and around the log pile. Elise and Oscar scrunched newspaper and threw it over the fire-guard.

I pulled out the round garden table and placed the squash on it. I had, the previous night, cut a jagged mouth with teeth in a smaller yellow squash and stuck it in one end as a mouth. Then I had added bulbous eyes made from tomatoes. The unveiling of the beginnings of the monster gathered attention quickly. I hardly needed to suggest that the beast might need wings, fire, a tail, for the troupe set about adding to it with glee.

Wearing our crowns of autumn remnants askew on our heads, we worked our hands over the squash, spiking leaves and seedpods and nutshells onto the green flesh with toothpicks. My late nights of wondering how to celebrate Michaelmas had paid off, and in the others' enthusiasm I saw the reflection of my own. We stood back to admire our fearsome creation, where it sat shaking its tongue, jagged and grinning above the forest floor that was adorned with the sheddings of trees—a beast of the harvest, come alive!

We gathered for song time, making a circle around the dragon. I had made up a song for Michaelmas, to be sung about each child and parent in turn complete with slaying actions and crossing the heart with the hands.

Slay the dragon, Cedar,
And build your strength for winter
You will find
that we will guide
and look after you!

As we sang, the trees still heavy and musty over us, it felt as if we were, indeed, ritually entering another season, a place of cold days and challenges, and that we were doing so together.

October

The woods were not quiet. And they were not, as one might expect in the month of October, ebbing towards winter, showing signs of dying, waning life. There was something of wakefulness and possibility throwing the yellow leaves of fruit trees and the copper acidity of the beeches about our heads as we climbed out of the car. The woods were excited and excitable! They reveled and wiggled in their splendor, in the unique way in which each piece met another to make a whole. How pleased the woods were with themselves!

On this particular morning we were making corn dollies with needle skirts. I had been saving corn-husks at home and drying them on the mantelpiece. In another woodland I had picked handfuls of long needles that had fallen from taller pines. They seemed the perfect length for corn doll skirts.

As I watched the parents working, I remembered with a twinge of embarrassment the mood I was in the night before when sitting down to invent the day's craft, to create the sample doll. When Joel asked me what I was doing I snapped at him, "Oh, some silly little thing." I was angry at myself. Why was I spending my time doing something so inconsequential? Why was I not able to fill my evenings with writing, with work? But during the twenty minutes it took me to make the sample doll and its fallen-needle skirt, a transformation of mood was set in motion. When it was finished I felt much happier. Now, in the woods, surrounded by others following the pattern, I thought about all the dolls going to their separate homes—not to last

Elise and Sue making a corn doll

long, no doubt, torn apart by a one zealous toddler or another, perhaps forgotten in the bottom of the woods bag, to be re-found the next week. Perhaps, if they were lucky, they would end up as part of a seasonal table or mantelpiece display. But the act of creating was full of meaning, memory, movement, shared discussion, the magical work of so many fingertips and eyes and minds. And the children were playing all around our tight crafting group. Were they watching? Were they aware of what we were doing?

The trees moaned overhead. No doubt, if one could decipher each sound, one could hear leaves falling, scraping their ragged edges against each other and us. Elise sat on Sue's lap, while Cedar moved around the edge of the crafting circle, clutching a handful of dried corn husks and talking to them or about them. The older boys moved logs and Oscar was asking for something to eat.

Oscar

16

November

Maxine, our new red cargo bike, arrived! Who would have thought that Lincolnshire had hills? In a car the small, gradual inclines and declines are not noticed. Maxine found them, and in turn my legs felt them. We rode her to the woods. How different a place can seem when one travels to it in a different way! Not only is the transportation and use of time different, but our actual route changed.

Once Cedar was buckled into the little bench seat in the large wooden box built into the front of the bike, packed in tightly with the array of woods necessities, we waved goodbye to Joel at the door and cycled through town. We took the old water railway that runs all the way from Lincoln to Boston. It runs down along the side of the Siemens factory and through an industrial car park. Then it takes a long, flat, rather bleak path on which I felt that we were very much alone even when we passed another cyclist and a dog walker. A few minutes later a sign, charting the water railways' history, indicated that we had reached Washingborough, and we crossed a puddled footbridge towards the village. The feeling of going in a direction that you do not know was overwhelming, especially in the cold, under the threat of dark clouds, running late, with a small child to keep warm and dry. In this state one forgets one's breathlessness, the aching limbs unused to such efforts.

After song time we hollowed out the pile of wet leaves and the children climbed in as if into a nest.

I pushed up a hill through Washingborough and into Heighton. If there is height in this part of the world, I felt we had gained it. A very wintry sun had battled it out with the clouds and bounced light off the road in front of us—bright, white light. I squinted and blinked across the open fields, which were visible over the short hedgerows and fences. I wondered if Cedar was doing the same. Her head was at an angle associated only with a state of deep relaxation. I considered she must be asleep. I sat up straight and felt wonderful: the cold, damp air in my face, the perfect white, magnified by the water settled on everything, the height, the speed, my fantastic thighs and the woods not far away now.

By the time we arrived, late and sweaty, the rain clouds had gathered force. After song time we hollowed out the pile of wet leaves around which we had sung and danced and the children climbed in, sitting there all together as if in a nest. I couldn't quite see their faces under hatted heads. Looking down at the ground, at the leaves and their feet in them, I could only imagine their expressions, ranging from delight, to uncertainty, from pleasure to wet discomfort and back again, not wondering at the world, for that, I believe, is an adult construct, but being in the woods, in the world.

By story time it was pouring and we all gathered in the shelter. There was very little room for all of us so we squeezed together, sharing our damp air. Jay ran to the compost toilet and brought back a lantern and a large candle, both of which were lit. "Light the little candle light. . . " we all sang, as the rain drummed out its own version on the canvas above our heads. I knelt down and began to tell the story. Peter and Lilly woke in their beds to the sound of rain on their windowpanes but they did not want to be cooped up all day long, so they ate their porridge, put on all their outdoor rain clothes, and went outside, opening their umbrellas in the garden. "Eeeeeee, pop!" Up went their umbrellas. Several little faces met me through the gathering gloom, illuminated by candlelight. There was restlessness, a feeling of uncomfortable wetness. My fingers were very cold. After a rather foreshortened woodland adventure, Peter and Lilly went home for tea and bed.

Autumn Songs and Crafts

Slay the Dragon
Words and music by Margaret Loescher

Slay the dra - gon, Ce - dar, and build your strength for win - ter.

You will find that we will guide and look af - ter you!

I'm a Tall, Tall, Tree

Words and music ©1979 Lorraine Lee Hammond, Snowy Egret Music, BMI
Lyrics adapted by Margaret Loescher; used by permission

This is my trunk, I'm a tall, tall tree. In the au-tumn the ap-ples

grow on me, and they drop. And they drop. This is my trunk, I'm a

tall, tall tree. In the win-ter the snow_ falls on me. And I shi-ver, and I

shi-ver. This is my trunk, I'm a tall, tall tree. In the spring time the blos-soms

grow on me. And they o-pen. And they o-pen. This is my trunk, I'm a

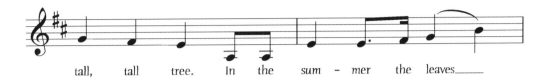

tall, tall tree. In the sum - mer the leaves____

grow on me. And they wave. And they wave.

Corn Dolls with Needle Skirts

1. Husk an ear of corn, separate the leaves, and dry it somewhere warm and light for one week. Save some of the silky hair and dry it, too. Collect some long pine needles.

2. Take a wide husk and fold it in half over your index finger. Remove your finger and press down on a firm surface to secure the fold. This will be the head and the body.

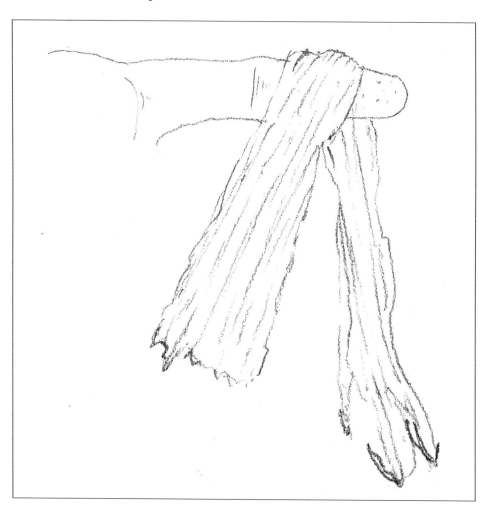

3. Take a shorter piece of husk and fold it in half, twisting it between your fingers to make it narrower. This will be the arms. Open out piece one and insert piece two, re-folding piece one over the top of piece two. The arms are now tucked inside the body.

4. Take a longer, narrower piece of husk and use it to tie the arms on to the body, leaving enough husk at the top to form the head. (Putting an index finger inside the fold that makes the head while a friend ties might help, or else use a stick or ruler.) Decide which side is the front of your doll and begin the tie from the back of the neck. Bring the tie to the front of the doll and cross it over the chest, wrapping underneath both armpits and then tying firmly at the back of the doll.

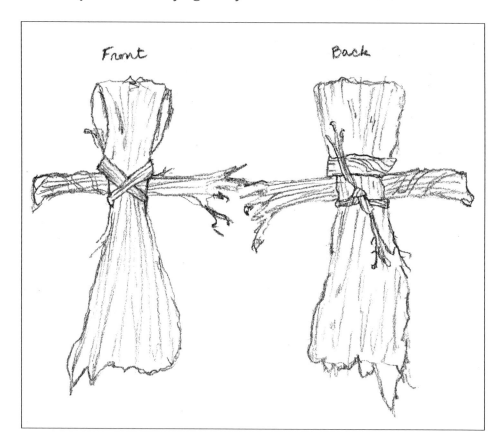

Front   Back

5. Give the head and skirt more width and form by gently pulling them wider.
6. Take the pine needles and, using another narrow piece of husk, tie one end of them around the doll's waist.
7. Use dried corn silk to stuff into the head and stick out the sides to look like hair.

1

2.

3.

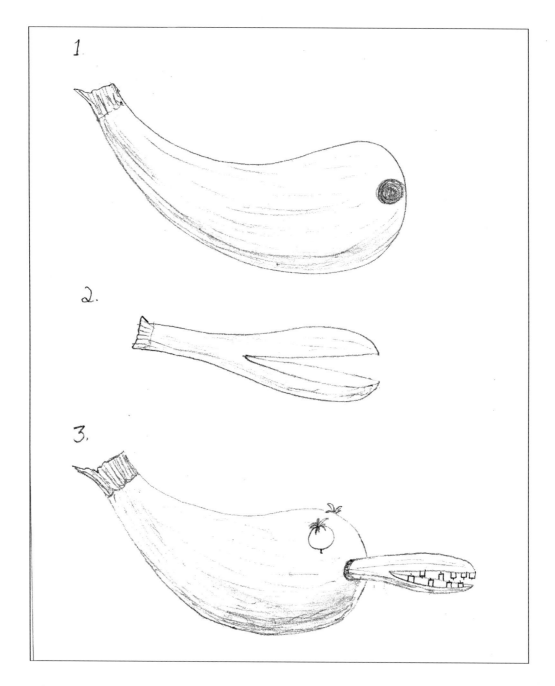

Squash Dragon

1. Grow or buy a very large, soft skinned squash. An over-grown zucchini or vegetable marrow works best. You will also need a smaller zucchini and two cherry tomatoes. Make a long horizontal cut down the middle of the smaller zucchini, but do not cut it to the end. Cut hole in the fat end of the larger zucchini, big enough to fit the small end of the smaller zucchini.

2. Insert small zucchini into large zucchini. Use toothpicks to attach cherry tomato "eyes." You can add kernels of corn for teeth or a thin slice of carrot or a long leaf for a tongue.

3. What can you find in the woods to attach to your dragon? Use toothpicks to attach leaves and pine cones. Sticks and feathers can usually be stuck into the squash's skin. Does your dragon have wings, a tail, feathers, spikes, scales, fire? Is it scary or friendly?

4.

Winter:
The Cold Wind Doth Blow

By the end of November the season had definitely changed. In the mornings there was mist in the woods, and often a white, winter light coming in low through the trees. Now came the cold, and with it a battling against the cold. Sitting on the ground for our picnic lunch had become uncomfortable and we left the willow dome for warmer months, gathering instead around the fire on chairs draped in blankets and sleeping bags. Still, on the coldest days there was discomfort reflected in the grumpiness of some of the children. Unfortunately the children's clothing available for sale in England is not up to winters in the woods. In Denmark, Holland, or Germany, where outdoor education is very popular and commonplace, woolen socks, warm waterproof trousers, and substantial coats are all widely available. So, too, is the mindset that goes with them, reflected so succinctly in the famous phrase, "There is no such thing as inappropriate weather, only inappropriate clothing." And to put our Englishness truly to the test in December, it snowed and snowed.

December

The snows began the day of the Alternative Christmas Market, at which the Lincolnshire Parent-and-Child Group had a stall. I had organized a crafting day at my house in November and had been making small felted fairies, bears in beds, Christmas cards, and tree ornaments for some weeks before that. Jay made several "bug hotels," hibernation

Left: Jay, Jenny D. and Oscar around the fire

Here were the woods transformed once again.

houses for insects. Jay, Sue, and I manned the stall. I had decided to use Maxine as our table-top and rigged up a beautiful display of felted delights emerging from the bike. Unfortunately the icy conditions kept potential buyers away and we sold very little. But the exercise helped unite the group in festive spirit.

To everyone's surprise the snow stayed and even gathered force. On the first Tuesday of the month I woke early and with enthusiasm for a magical white morning in the woods, I re-worked a poem about rain into one about snow.

It is all white in the woods today
Wrapped in a thick wool blanket
All night long it fell with a muffled, snuffled sound.
I saw it in my dreams and when I woke as well,
All across the fields and hills
And thick upon my windowsill.

Of course, we took the car and as I drove through virgin snow into the woods I was too full of spirit to worry about how—or if—we were to get out again. No one had been in the woods since the last snow and we paced out, our boots creaking, definite and bold into the stillness, with the heaviness of the ground below us and the weighted canopy above our heads. A bird called and the layers of white absorbed the sound, making it brief, hugging it close. How is it that snow muffles sound? Is it because each sound stands alone, unique because there are so few of them, everything too heavy to move? Is it because, like soft furnishings in an echoing house, the snow absorbs all sounds? Or is it simply because we whisper, in awe of something so strange? Here were the woods transformed once again.

No one else arrived. I built a snowman. Cedar took very little interest in it. The snow, as deep as her boots, seemed to baffle her and it challenged her movement too much for comfort. Eventually she found a stick and took some pleasure in making holes in the snow while I found some woodland treasures to make the snowman's face. Even when the snowman was finished she hardly noticed it. I felt sorry that we were not a group on this magical morning. Perhaps Cedar would be more adventurous with other children around.

I decided to follow through with the story and we sat wrapped in blankets in the shelter. Peter and Lilly woke to find a world covered in white. They dressed warmly and set out for a woodland adventure to build a snowman. I reached down and picked up real snow, packing it into small snowballs. At the end of the story Cedar requested I tell it again. I refused a third time and then Cedar wanted to walk over and see the snowman that she had taken so little interest in earlier. She began talking about it and even

Shelter in the focal clearing

began touching it and the snow around it, holding it in her hand, pressing it together as I had done in the story. We stayed for a while longer, reforming the snowman's face together, and when I felt it was time to go (the snow was falling heavily now and I was worried about being able to get the car out on to the road) it was Cedar who wanted to stay, knee deep in the snow. The story, it was clear to me, had enabled her to embrace the transformation of the woods.

We only just made it home before the blizzard hit Lincoln. We were snowed in for a week. Icy conditions ensued and the woodland group was cancelled three weeks in a row. We are not in Denmark after all.

January

All five mothers were on fire duty, struggling to light the fire with wet kindling and on damp, cold ground. Three were collecting wood, one had matches in hand, and the fifth was fanning with determination. On our fourth or fifth attempt to light it, Onyx started singing, leaning towards the fire and making up a strange high-pitched song without formed words. He continued for some time, seemingly driven by some instinctual need and in his own world as if he were meditating and eventually the fire lit!

I wanted to start song time with a new poem I had written just that morning.

> *When it is cold and wintery wet,*
> *I like to take a walk and wear my hat.*
> *We gather wood from the trees all around,*
> *And drag it home upon the ground.*
> *We use our axe to chop it up,*
> *And build a fire after our sup.*
> *All the wood of different sizes,*
> *Light a match and the smoke rises!*
> *It keeps us warm all through the night,*
> *What a wonderful, bright, bright light.*

> **We added in handfuls of moss, heavy with yesterday's rain, and tied it all together with very fine copper wire.**

The craft activities in nature's meager months tended to involve rather a lot of materials gathered from elsewhere. Likewise the task to find things to include in the story was not met with such glee by the children but rather little faces that seemed to say, "Well, what is there?" and I was handed the odd wet stick or handful of rotting leaf mold. However, there was always the most amazing dense, dark green moss in the woods that became ever more accessible and visible against the general browns of the other hibernating vegetation. This moss was often included in the story and was also essential to this January morning's craft. Having not fully completed the winter wreath craft I had introduced right before Christmas, we continued it using old wire coat hangers no longer needed at my house, tentacles of ivy growing in my garden, pieces of holly cut off a fallen tree I found in the pre-Christmas snows, and pine cones I collected in some other woods in November and dried so that they popped open. We added in handfuls of moss, heavy with yesterday's rain, and tied it all together with very fine copper wire from Jenny's old television set. Our fingers soon got too cold to work the tentacles of green around the wire and the project slowed to a halt with a general consensus to continue the following week.

Sometimes the whining from the cold rippled through the group, toppling one little soul after another like dominoes. I hoped it would not take hold but it was indeed cold, colder than it seemed earlier in the morning, and the wind had picked up. We swiftly moved towards lunch by the fire. This time there were so few of us that we could sit around the little round garden table easily. We dragged it into a patch of weak sun that had thankfully appeared. I had brought warm water for hand-washing but had not quite got the temperature right and the thermos had kept it very hot, indeed, so we poured it into the bowl to let it cool. The children held their faces over the billowing steam and cold little hands dipped in and received a rush of warmth: a treat from a faraway land of gas heating and electric kettles. I had brought baked beans in a thermos for a hot treat, too. Everyone ate heartily.

On the woodland wander Kai wanted to use the wheelbarrow and Paula helped him. They filled it up with lots of moss and sticks. Kai was quite certain he had collected a ladybug for the story and wanted to make sure I included it in the telling. In the story Peter and Lilly climbed a tree, looking back at their house, the river, the swan. When they passed the swan its head was tucked under its wing like the robin in the song:

The cold wind doth blow and we shall have snow
And what will the robin do then, poor thing?
He'll fly into a barn and keep himself warm
And tuck his head under his wing, poor thing.

Peter and Lilly took a handful of seeds as they left their house and put them on the garden bench for the birds:

Four little seeds, sitting on a bench,
"Thank you," said the blackbird,
"Those will do for lunch!"
He ate numbers one and two,
Then he ate number three
And once he'd eaten number four
There were none left to see!

At the end of the story during the lullaby for Peter and Lilly Kai was saying something repeatedly to his mother, Paula. "He's asking for the ladybug!" Oh, no! I had forgotten the ladybug, perhaps because there was no actual prop and it was completely out of season! Kai looked quite upset so I pretended that I suddenly found a little ladybug under the moss still on the table. All three little children jumped off their chairs and out of their blankets and came running over and gathered in a semi-circle around the table, their faces turned down, mesmerized by my wiggling little finger, the ladybug. The ladybug said hello to all of them each in turn and tickled Kai on the nose. He seemed very satisfied. "That would make such a wonderful picture," said Jenny "all of them there, like that." And I had a sudden feeling of a divided self: the one who might have taken the photograph, lying outside of the action and the joy of witnessing the little three in awe, watching them watching me, or rather watching my finger, a thing almost detached from me, indeed, a different beast, a ladybug, and then also being myself in the unplanned moment, in the spontaneity of the story, being the pretend, falling into my own imagination and joining with the little three as one being through that. The ego, the joining, the imagination. How could all of these be met in a single unplanned moment?

Winter Poems, Songs, and Crafts

White in the Woods Today

Margaret Loescher, with inspiration from the poem "Everything's Wet"
by Jean Kenward

> *It is all white in the woods today*
> *Wrapped in a thick wool blanket*
> *All night long it fell with a muffled, snuffled sound.*
> *I saw it in my dreams and when I woke as well,*
> *All across the fields and hills*
> *And thick upon my windowsill.*

When it is Cold

Margaret Loescher

> *When it is cold and wintery wet,*
> *(hug yourself and shiver)*
> *I like to take a walk and wear my hat.*
> *(mime putting on a hat)*
> *We gather wood from the trees all around,*
> *(mime picking up sticks and make canopy of tree overhead with hands)*
> *And drag it home upon the ground.*
> *(mime dragging a large stick along the ground)*
> *We use our axe to chop it up,*
> *(mime holding and using an axe)*
> *And build a fire after our sup.*
> *(mime placing logs on top of each other)*
> *All the wood of different sizes,*
> *(show different lengths of imaginary wood with both hands)*
> *Light a match and the smoke rises!*
> *(mime lighting a match and reach both arms up to the sky for the rising smoke)*
> *It keeps us warm all through the night,*
> *(gently and slowly fold arms across chest, laying both hands flat on chest)*
> *What a wonderful, bright, bright light.*

Four Little Seeds
Adapted from the traditional rhyme "Four Little Berries"

Four little seeds, sitting on a bench,
"Thank you," said the blackbird,
"Those will do for lunch!"
He ate numbers one and two,
Then he ate number three
And once he'd eaten number four
There were none left to see!

The Cold Wind Doth Blow
Traditional

The cold wind doth blow_ and we shall have snow, and what will the ro-bin do

then, poor thing? He'll sit in a barn_ and keep him-self warm, and

hide his head un - der his wing, poor thing.

Winter Wreath

1.   Take a wire coat hanger and pull down on the middle of the lower part to create a diamond shape.
2.   Wind a long piece of ivy around the coat hanger.
3.   Use thin wire or green string to tie other plants to the hanger. Moss, holly, and pinecones work well. Finish off with a ribbon bow if you want to.

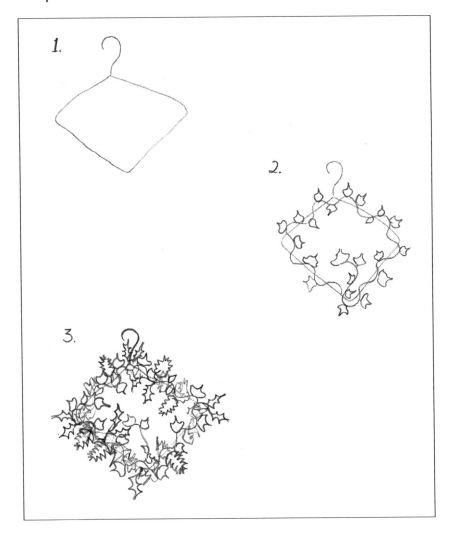

Bark Boats

1. Collect thick pieces of bark. Large conifers are the best trees for such bark. Find a straight twig. Make a small hole in the bark and insert the end of the twig. You now have your boat and your mast.

2. Take a small piece of thin material (an old hanky works well) and cut a triangular shape. Tie, sew or glue it to itself over the mast. Attach the other end of the material to the boat by tucking it into a crevice in the bark or gluing it.

Early Spring: Naked Woodland Feet

January

In our bed, in a sleepy morning daze, I heard Joel telling Cedar about it being the Jewish New Year for Trees. I thought I had perhaps dreamed it so over breakfast I asked Joel about it. Yes, it was true! There was a New Year celebration for trees in the Jewish calendar. I thought that was a perfect thing for our woods group to celebrate. After all, we had reached the time of year when the sap starts to rise in the trees, marking the beginning of their season of growth. Aside from the importance of trees, the festival celebrates our connection to each other, to the earth, and to the Source of life.

In the summer we had made a tree decoration around the lower reaches of the trunk of one of the large beech trees that border the woodland clearing, taking bundles of wool and tying the top ends to the trunk. We had used it as a Maypole, each taking a string and dancing around the tree, pulling the string over and under the other dancers and their strings. The end pattern was not terribly successful, but we had a funny tangle. I decided it was time to have another go at this. Joel picked up some rolls of yarn on his way home from work and I learned a lovely tree song from Jane. It is usually sung as a round and it goes like this:

Left: Sue, Elsie and Cedar with snowdrops

Trees grow tall in the heart of the forest,
High in the sky!
While the roots grow down in the deep, dark earth.

I incorporated into it some nice big stretching up and down movements for the children to take part in.

With dry kindling brought from our homes the fire started easily and was roaring by the time everyone else arrived. It began to rain lightly and we all took cover under the tent while we drank our tea and ate our fruit bites. There was a snug feeling of camaraderie and a relaxation with the warmer weather. I could tell it was going to be a lovely group today. I introduced the New Year for Trees idea and as soon as the rain let up we all took off, very enthusiastically, to the tree I had chosen. Jenny D. said it was a chestnut and showed me how the buds were already sticky with sap. Each of the children chose a ball of wool, and after a little discussion about the formation of the dance, off we went! We sang to the tune of *Here We Go Round the Mulberry Bush*:

> *This is the way we wrap our tree, wrap our tree, wrap our tree*
> *This is the way we wrap our tree, to celebrate its growth!*

We wound the colored yarn. It did not make a pattern of any real sense, but it looked pretty. Then we gave up on following a formation and I suggested the children just run around the tree with the yarn, wrapping more color about it, which they seemed to enjoy. The sun had come out and caught the smoke billowing across the clearing and off into the atmosphere. All the tree-wrappers were back-dropped in dusty, white light. I pulled out the bag of pinecones and lengths of ivy and holly that we had been using for our winter wreaths the weeks before and we used them to tuck into the yarn. We all worked on the decorating at our own pace and in our own ways. I noticed the children started having little conversations with themselves, with each other and their mothers and with the tree about it being a new year. This made me smile. When all the decorating items were used we stood back and

There was a snug feeling of camaraderie and a relaxation with the warmer weather.

admired it. Then we gave the tree some hugs and wished it a good year of growth and health.

Wrapping the tree with colored yarn to celebrate the New Year for Trees

Circle time followed. We sang all the usual songs and then we joined hands around the tree and sang the song Jane had taught me the day before.

After our picnic we went for a wander into the woods just beyond the willow dome and looked for snowdrops where they grew in abundance last year. We sang the new snowdrop song as we looked in the mossy, leaf-strewn ground, deep and moist and dark, where the tree-roots meet, tangle, and un-meet again. There they were, the little drops of white! They were hanging down, modestly, but with great purpose, amongst their spiky green foliage. They were still very small and we could sense that there were many more that had not yet appeared so we trod carefully.

Snowdrop, snowdrop, little drops of snow
What do you do when the cold wind blows?
We bow our little heads and say:
"Cold wind, cold wind, go away!"
Snowdrop, snowdrop, little drops of white
What do you do when the sun shines bright?
We ring our little bells and say:
"Ding-a-ling ding-a-ling, here comes spring!"

Elise was crouched down, bottom almost touching the ground, and I could see Sue's fingers next to hers, gently stroking the tops of the flower and talking softly, in her way, under her breath. Jenny G., too, was next to Onyx and Jenny D. was looking at another family of snowdrops with Oscar. I was so interested in how the discovery of the little flowers had separated off the mother-child pairs into their units and crouched them down into the moss, that I did not notice Cedar de-heading and closely examining hers as she pulled one petal off at a time! "Soft!" She said very enthusiastically. "Oh, ho! Touch but don't pick!" I reached down to touch the flower delicately.

In the story that day, when Lilly climbed the tree she saw the sticky buds on the ends of the branches.

February

At the beginning of February the weather had warmed up and we took to eating seated on the canvas on the ground in the willow dome. I had been given some air-drying clay and we rolled it out into wide, thin sheets and made leaf imprints. Onyx found a very big leaf and made a fantastic press with his Mum. I was noticing more and more how much older than the other children he was. I knew that in the summer I would notice age differences even more. In the winter it all seemed evened out by the layers of clothing. But I noticed it when I washed their hands—what different-sized hands they had!

Despite the warmer weather, fire building seemed to characterize much of the month. For a while, with Jay away, we stumbled in our efforts but in February it improved and a rhythm was set up around it. I seemed to have my hands too full to build the fire, what with arriving, unpacking the bike, getting Cedar out and on the potty peacefully, welcoming people and making cups of tea. Sue took this task on graciously and without announcement in her quiet and determined manner. She was very good at it. Jenny G. and Onyx found wood from the woodpile or amongst the nearby trees, depending on recent weather. And a craft activity was formed: wood collecting and sawing! It started one

Despite the warmer weather, fire building seemed to characterize much of the month.

Monday evening when I felt too lethargic to bring myself to create a craft and so, with a feeling of failure, threw a wood saw into the bike and considered we could do with replenishing our wood supplies. In the damp months we had used a lot of wood from the wood pile and we ought to have been regularly re-stocking it. It turned out to be the perfect activity for the morning, and Jenny G., Sue, and I took turns using the saw while the children collected large pieces of fallen branches in the wheelbarrow. We had recently had a spell of heavy winds and then dry weather so that there was quite a bit of wood to be found. The activity kept us all warm and had a real purpose. Jenny G. and Sue both said how much they enjoyed it. We repeated it later in the month.

We could not quite work out whether the fire kept us warm at all or simply provided psychological warmth. It certainly made us all smell of smoke. I loved smelling Cedar's hair on a Tuesday night. It smelt like woods and fire smoke and reminded me of how far we had traveled that day, what a distant place we had been in, and how lucky we were to be cozy and warm inside now that it was dark.

On one February morning, after the story and the goodbye song, when some had already parted from the woods, Cedar sat on her potty amongst the deep smell of leaves slowly turning into earth and began to take off her lower clothes. I was in conversation with Jenny G. at the time and so did not notice until Cedar was wandering deeper into the trees, naked, poking holes in the earth with a stick. "Look! Making holes, making holes, Mummy!" Onyx thought this was most humorous and followed her around giggling. I have heard from several sources how the spring can bring on "the crazies" in animals and young children: stripping down, rolling around in spring grass, biting the air, a basic need to commune with nature, skin to skin, a digesting of all the energies now beginning on their upward journey towards the cosmos. How do we catch it all as it runs past us? I thought about all the things I could do as a leader to engage the children and parents in the seasonal changes. What songs should I be singing now? Were winter songs still appropriate? Could they be mixed with springy-er ones or would that confuse? What craft activities could we do when the woods were all about potential and yet had very little left in them by way of crafting resources? And here, in an act of naked defiance, unannounced, bestial, unconscious, was my answer. How little you can, oh Leader, lead! Spring was coming! Here it was in these naked woodland feet.

Early Spring Songs and Crafts

Trees Grow Tall
Traditional

Trees grow tall in the heart of the for - est, high in the sky, while the roots grow down in the deep, dark earth.

Snowdrop Song

Author unknown

Snow drops, snow drops, lit - tle drops of snow, What do you do when the
cold winds blow? We bow our lit-tle heads and say, Cold wind, cold wind, go a -
way. Snow drops, snow drops, lit - tle drops of white,
What do you do when the sun shines bright? We ring our lit-tle bells and
say, Ding - a - ling, Ding - a - ling, here comes spring!

Hairy Pinecones

1. Collect pinecones and store them on a radiator until they dry and pop open. Collect some earth and moss and place in a shallow container, standing the pinecone up in the middle. Sprinkle a little grass seed between the scales of the cone.

2. Keep the cone and moss moist by spraying it with water daily and keeping it away from direct heat. When kept moist the cone scales should close again and the grass seed should begin to grow, leaving a sprouting, green pinecone in your miniature garden!

Spring: Catch It If You Can!

March

The light began to warm everything.

What a glorious day it was! Not a cloud was in sight and the Lincolnshire big sky had grown even bigger. There had been a slight frost overnight and a cold wind blew against us as we struggled to the woods. Winter was not giving up easily. The bike was very heavy, full of things to make pancakes on the open fire: a large wooden mixing bowl, two wooden spoons, a large frying pan, a spatula spoon for turning the pancakes, silverware, margarine, vegan pancake mix, soy milk, maple syrup, dish towels, a pot lid for keeping the pancake stack warm while more cooked, and a wire grate from one of my oven shelves to balance on bricks either side of the flames. I had to run through the list of needs in my head several times the night before. I had thought that combining the craft activity and the lunch would lessen the load—what a mistake! But I had promised pancakes the week before, and was determined to make it work. And once I had slogged it out and reached the woods, I was so glad I had persevered.

The light began to warm everything. The buds on the trees were catching it, the waning snowdrops were catching it, the tops of the shelters were catching it, the bits of found glass and stone on the woodland altar were catching it, and everything seemed to glow and to sigh. A few weeks earlier we had noticed that the willow-weave fireguard had started to sprout. It was

Left: Jay on pancake duty

still alive! There was definitely an appropriate feeling of change and festivity in the air.

Jay and Archie finally came back. We had missed their presence these last two months. Jay embraced the fire building once again. Archie, Onyx and Cedar tried on each other's hats until the others arrived: Jenny D. and Oscar and and Kai came for a drop-in. Jenny D. stood in the clearing looking up into the light. Her pregnancy bump was now very big.

The order of events had to be altered in order to bring together the craft and the lunch (the cooking and the eating of the pancakes.) That meant that circle time was to come first. On this day it was helped by Jay and Archie's renewed enthusiasm and the pancake rhyme:

Mix a pancake,
Stir a pancake,
Pop it in the pan;
Fry the pancake,
Toss the pancake–
Catch it if you can!

Above: Cedar, Onyx and Oscar on mixing duty; opposite, Oscar, Onyx, Cedar and Archie on eating duty

And then the pancakes themselves. I placed the large bowl on the bench and with the two wooden spoons, the children took turns (in twos) mixing the

Jay even managed to toss one (and catch it again!) much to the delight of the children.

batter. The old saying, "Too many cooks spoil the broth," did not apply. Once the batter was mixed, the adults, too, worked together beautifully. I was manning the batter and the frying pan and cooking the pancakes, Jay was looking after the fire, Jenny D. had set up a feeding station and was preparing already-cooked pancakes, adorning them with maple syrup and fruit and handing them out to the children who were sitting in a lovely line on a bench in the sun, waiting eagerly and watching the fire. Then we all swapped in and out of the various tasks in order to each have a moment to eat our own pancakes.

After the first bunch, which cooked a little too quickly, the flames died down and the glowing ashes made for much better pancakes. The second batch was a perfect golden brown and the best I have ever made. Jay even managed to toss one (and catch it again!) much to the delight of the children.

On our cycle home along the canal I noticed that the sunlight that had been, on previous days, coming through the bare tree branches and hitting my eyes like a strobe as we sped past, was now high enough in the sky to shine on us uninterrupted.

April

At the beginning of the month Joel's university notified its staff of imminent job cuts. It seemed there was a strong possibility that Joel would no longer have a job come September. This meant we might need to depart from Lincoln and leave the woodland group behind. I wanted to voice this possibility to the Lincolnshire Group in order to help them prepare for finding a new leader, but at the same time I did not want it to unsettle our group in the woods too early. It was a tricky balance to maintain and, as a consequence, I often felt at odds with myself during our April woodland adventures.

When we did meet our group was very small, but numbers were boosted by a couple of visits. Laura and her one-year-old Henry whom we knew from the other parent-and-child group came along. It was interesting how the presence of a crawling child changed the group dynamic. Luckily it was dry and I spread the large tarpaulin and blanket on the ground near the fire and we did our crafts at ground level. I had learned a song about hibernating animals waking up for spring and I began to act it out, crouched down low, no doubt influenced by Henry's height. Our other visitor who became a regular was a 94-year-old man named Don. Don knew pretty much everyone there was to know in certain Lincoln circles and seemed, in the short time that I knew him, to be a social glue, the foundation of several communities if not embodying the very sense of community. Don was

> Perhaps it was the children's sensing of what we had created together that allowed for a certain development in imaginative play.

an old friend of Jane and Nick Wise and knew Heartwood. I knew Don from Quaker Meeting and when I first told him about our parent-and-child group his eyes lit up. "As soon as I get a break from my Art History classes, I'll come along. I've got lots of wood for the fire." And sure enough, come April Don turned up with a car full of wood. On the first occasion of his visit he arrived an hour and a half early, unloaded his wood, built a roaring fire and tidied the focal clearing, all before we pulled up on Maxine. He had also brought along paper and his origami skills. So as I made tissue paper butterflies on the tarpaulin with Laura and Henry, Don showed anyone who was interested how to make origami peace birds.

Don continued to attend when he could throughout May, June and July. He participated in circle time, dancing enthusiastically. His presence indicated to me how this group in Heartwoods had become so much more than a parent-and-child group. It had become a circle of friends of various ages, who came to be in the woods but also to be with one another.

Perhaps it was the children's sensing of what we had created together, combined with the onslaught of spring, that allowed for a certain development in imaginative play. At free play time the children developed a woodland kitchen game in which they used the pots and pans and kettles left in the woods for cooking on the fire and filled them with leaves, moss, and water and then served them to the parents. It was special cuisine that continued in some form for weeks. They also developed a game called "Manager Helper," during which a space was guarded by one or two children and the only way for the others to get past was for them to announce that they were the "manager-helper." I could not quite believe that being in such a beautiful natural environment could inspire such a corporate game! Perhaps it was a reflection of their need to assert control over this very big, wild place.

May

May, the month of green. Suddenly the woods had changed and the new season was upon us. Each leaf, opened and receiving, added to the shade over our heads. The sky disappeared into the realm of the imagined and its light waited for the wind to part its barrier and shatter down, momentarily, never still, never peaceful. We sought it out, that light, the air still cold, and sat in its quivering, the hairs on our arms and legs alert, the skin surprised in its whiteness.

In April I had applied for a job as a kindergarten assistant at the Cambridge Steiner School. The Cambridge School was pioneering in its outdoor kindergarten work and this appealed to me. By the middle of May I was offered the job and while nothing else had materialized for either of us, and Cambridge was a familiar and well-loved city, I accepted the position. And thus our departure from Lincoln was set in motion. We would leave in the middle of July.

> **Families gathered, bits of colored ribbon littered around them, small bells tinkling in children's hands.**

I worried about the continuation of the group in my absence and so, in the hopes of introducing new families to Heartwood, I suggested a May Day gathering and fund-raiser. I had a simple May pole made by my mother from a thick bamboo pole and I had several handfuls of ribbons and bells. That seemed enough to begin.

On the day of the May celebration I began by nervously busying myself with setting up the fund-raising stall and the craft activity, seeking out the occasional sunny patches on the woodland floor. Then the families began to arrive and they continued arriving until we had quite a crowd. There was a need for a gathering after all! I noticed, moving about from one task to another, that there was a certain understanding that passed between the Heartwoods regulars, expressed in an excited glance as we passed each other in the crowd. How marvelous it was to host a party here in the place where we felt we belonged!

The lunches were turned out and we all held hands for our blessing, making a big web across numerous picnic blankets. The stall selling handmade crafts was already doing some business and raffle tickets were being sold for a hamper that we had collected together. After lunch I gave out the craft activity. It was little elasticated ribbon and bell armbands for jangling around the May Pole. Families gathered, bits of colored ribbon littered around them, small bells tinkling in children's hands. Then we had circle time. I had worried about how to gather together such a large group in one circle. A friend and I began singing and pretty soon others joined us and then still more until the children and the parents squeezed together in the clearing. It was interesting to see how ingrained in them, children and parents alike, was the response to the call to song.

The final song, "Dance Away, Dance Away!" began the procession, which Jane and I led, holding high a branch of hawthorn covered in small white flowers. We led the group away from the focal clearing and along the path that weaves under the new trees, past the birdbath full of special stones and shells brought to life under the magnifying properties of water, and through to the stage, in front of which Joel had earlier stuck the May Pole deep into the earth. Finding it there, adorned with flowing ribbons, deep in the heart of the woods, was like something out of a dream. Then Jane taught two new songs for us to sing as the children danced and we did a very basic weave, under, over, under, over. We had no instruments other than our bells and so we encouraged all the parents to sing as heartily as they could. The sound resounded through the new undergrowth. As we attempted to reverse the dance and unwind the ribbons we got in a tangle, laughed a lot, and gave up for cake and juice sold from the stage to small, enthusiastic purchasers, the coins warm from their hands. We had welcomed new faces into the woods and together with them we had welcomed May into the woods.

Spring Poems, Songs, and Crafts

Pancake Rhyme

Christina Rossetti

Mix a pancake,
Stir a pancake,
Pop it in the pan;
Fry the pancake,
Toss the pancake–
Catch it if you can!

Here's a Branch of Snowy May

Traditional Dutch

Music from *The Singing Year* by Candy Verney (Hawthorn Press, 2006)

Here's a branch of snow - y may, a branch the fair - ies gave us.

Who would like to dance to-day, with the branch the fair-ies gave us? Dance a-way,

dsance a - way, hold - ing high the branch of may. Dance a - way,

dance a - way, hold - ing high the branch of may.

Wake Up!

Words by Nicola Wicksteed, Music by Candy Verney
From *The Singing Year* by Candy Verney (Hawthorn Press, 2006)

I'm a dor mouse; I've slept the win-ter through. Curled up in my nest, I've

slept the win-ter through. Come the spring-time This is what I do: WAKE UP!_

Scrab-ble scrab-ble here, scrab-ble scrab-ble there, look-ing for my food,

scrab - ble scrab - ble scrab - ble scrab - ble ev - ery where!

I'm a green frog;
I've slept the winter through.
Underneath the mud,
I've slept the winter through.
Come the springtime
This is what I do:

WAKE UP! Jumping jumping here
Jumping jumping there,
looking for my food,
Jumping jumping jumping jumping
Everywhere!

I'm a small bat;
I've slept the winter through.
Hanging in the barn,
I've slept the winter through.
Come the springtime
This is what I do:

WAKE UP! Flitter flitter here
Flitter flitter there,
looking for my food,
Flitter flitter flitter flitter
Everywhere!

Tissue Paper Butterflies

1. Using two different colors of tissue paper, one on top of the other, cut out a wide butterfly shape from both pieces. These are the wings. (If you are making butterflies with very young children you can simplify the design by using a double layer rectangle of tissue paper rather than the template below.)

2. Take a pipe cleaner and fold it in half. Insert the tissue paper between the two halves of the pipe cleaner, making sure that the folded end of the pipe cleaner is at the back end of the butterfly. The pipe cleaner is the body of the butterfly.

3. Gently gather the tissue paper, giving the wings some wrinkles. Twist the pipe cleaner at both ends to secure it on to the wings. At the front end of the butterfly, make your twist further down the body, leaving the two ends of the pipe cleaner as antennae.

4. To give the butterfly depth and a sense of movement, bend the pipe cleaner slightly and gently separate the two different colors of tissue paper wings. Thread a needle and thread once around the middle of the body of the butterfly. Tie off and leave the thread long. Find a twig and attach the thread to it. Your butterfly can flutter and float on the end of your twig!

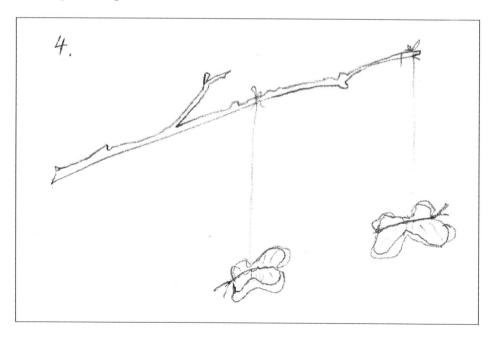

Summer:
Fire Bread

June

June, lovely June,
That beautifies the ground!
The song of the cuckoo through the green woods
resounds!

I had wanted May to last forever. The dry, warm spring had brought on flowers rapidly and sent them to seed quickly. By June many of the early summer flowers were over and the heavy feeling of July or August was already upon us. In the woods nettles grew as high as the children and we battled them down in our willow dome. Our group in June was again altered. In the second week of May, Jenny D. had her baby and so she no longer attended with Oscar. And Sue and Elise did not come for a few weeks because of work and social commitments. We were, however, blessed with Joel's company now that his university term was over. Laura and Henry also continued to come when they could and Laura expressed an interest in taking over the running of the group when I left. Don, too, came along often. By the middle of the month two new families had joined us, each consisting of a mother and one eighteen month old. We spent most of the month preparing for two festivals, Whitsun and Saint John's.

Throughout the year I had been often asked directly about the seasonal festivals, or else felt the need to email parents ahead of time and offer explanations. I offered a simplified version of the Christian message, the manner in which the timing and theme of the festival might coincide

Left: Cedar in body paint

63

with other religious festivals as well as its more pagan attributes, and how the festival reflected and celebrated the season and was, indeed, relevant to our group in the woods. Michaelmas had been relatively straightforward with the image of a dragon, a harvest, an act of bravery and preparing for the winter to come. Christmas was so ingrained it was almost self-explanatory with its cold, hard earth, its deep heart, its tiny baby, and various religious festivals of light. Easter for one reason or another had slipped past our group in the woods, but once again, there was a deep cultural understanding of this festival reflected so beautifully in the newness of growth. And Saint John's was easy to explain. The headiness of summer was upon us, life on earth had grown out as far into the cosmos as it could stretch, emotions uncontrolled, heads without sense, and all this reflected in the fire. But what of Whitsun? I read about it for some time before the event but it still baffled me. There was something almost too

Our Whitsun dove wreath

transcendental about it. The complications of sacrifice and new life carried over from Easter, and the ascent of Christ was something too complicated for me, let alone children. Luckily no one asked me about Whitsun. Perhaps they unconsciously already knew what it was about, as if it had seeped into them. I, too, hoped that would happen to me as I made my dove wreath and laid out my white clothes.

For a while everyone sat crouched by the fire, looking at their bread, very quiet under the high trees.

On our cycle ride to the Whitsun picnic Joel, Cedar and I scoured the river banks for white blooms. The hawthorn was over. All that was left was large wild daisies. We picked a handful along with long grasses gone to seed. At the woods we spread a white cloth on the little round garden table and put the grasses in a cup. I hung up the Whitsun wreath that we had collectively made over the last two weeks. The doves which, having been made by different hands on different occasions, were a collection of shapes and sizes, flew about in the breeze.

I was pleased to see that Jay had remembered to dress Archie and Onyx in white. The day was not yet warm but the sun was out and making what had now become its familiar pattern on the woodland floor. Jay sought out its rays, pulling himself on to the large fallen tree that marked the edge of the central fire area. Joel, Cedar and the boys soon followed. They sat in a row up on the fallen tree, the men closing their eyes and putting their faces up towards the sky, the children engaged in stick or stone, looking down into their laps or towards one another.

Two evenings before I had made a simple white bread dough, stretchy and moist, something akin to pizza dough, and I had rolled it in cling wrap and put it in the fridge. Now I placed breadboards and flour on the table and started to roll pieces of the dough into long thin snake shapes. I soon had three helpers, working their small hands into the texture. I began to find appropriate sticks, at least three feet long and hefty enough not to burn when held over the fire. Jay, Joel and I stripped the ends of the sticks with penknives. Once the bread was long and narrow, we wound the bread around the clean ends of the sticks, squeezing it to stop it falling off. Now we had sticks with bread coils at the ends. Offering careful supervision we lifted the children over the fireguard and they sat down by the burning embers and small flames holding their sticks and fire bread over the heat and turning them slowly. For a while everyone sat crouched by the fire, looking at their bread, very quiet under the high trees. It took rather a long time for the bread to cook and the children began to get hot faces and lose interest. We rigged up a few bricks on either side of the fire and laid the sticks across them, Jay turning them constantly, while the children played amongst the trees.

We ate our snack in the willow dome, under the dove wreath and on our white tablecloth. We tore apart our fire bread coils and shared them. Some parts were quite charred, others perfectly white

Onyx and Archie and Cedar rolling out the dough

and fluffy with a fire crust. Then the children pulled the remaining pieces from the sticks with their teeth. How good it was to eat something hot from our very own fire!

Two weeks later, for St. John's, we made fire masks using red, orange and yellow paper and pieces of wool. The tops of the masks extended over the children's heads and

The children loved their masks and jumped around, roaring like flames.

in the paper we cut long flame-like patterns. The children loved their masks and jumped around, roaring like flames. It seemed to work as an alternative to jumping a fire, something I was not comfortable encouraging with such little children. We all wore our masks as we danced at circle-time. We sang a new song, and jumped an imaginary fire, the pile of rotting leaves always at the centre of our circle time, left over from autumn days.

'Dressing up' in the focal clearing

Fire Child dance, Fire Child sing, Fire Child you are mine!
Fire Child dance, Fire Child sing, Fire Child you are mine!
Light streaming, light streaming, watching my Fire Child grow!
Light streaming, light streaming, watching my Fire Child grow!

In the June story Peter and Lilly built a tent in the woods, using long sticks and very large leaves, wider than the children's faces. They padded out the floor of their tent with moss to sleep on. They carefully built a fire and cooked their dinner on it. As night fell they climbed into their tent, with their heads sticking out so that they could see the star-filled sky.

Star light, star bright,
First star I see tonight,
Wish I may, wish I might,
Have the wish I wish tonight!

The children were enthralled. Summer was at its height.

At the end of the month we did actually camp out in the woods. Only a few of us were able to come. We erected three tents under the canopy, avoiding the big roots of the beech trees. I do not think I have ever camped somewhere so familiar, discounting, of course, my own garden. It seemed to make sense, allowing ourselves a deeper understanding of the place. We could now see darkness creep into these woods and then lightness rise up out of them again. We cooked dinner on the fire, taking turns to man the soup in the crock, the veggie sausages above the flames, and talking about many different things. The afternoon had been overcast and heavy, but in the evening the sun pierced through the trees, electric, and a magnificent sunset illuminated the trunks, orange, like stage lights. Only some individual leaves had shadows, perfect and sharp, the rest grouped into night.

July

The month of our house move was finally upon us. In between clearing out and packing up, I frantically made felt swans for each of the children at Heartwood. I copied the swan I used for the story, which was originally made somewhere in Mongolia. White felt filled my days and my dreams. Very small stitches made a fine job of it, and I stuffed each one with combed wool so their necks stood firm and curved and proud just like the swan in the story. In the final two weeks, as and when the regular children attended, I emotionally gave them away, feeling as I did so how important it was to have marked the occasion with a physical object in which was embodied the same reverence with which Peter and Lilly bowed to the swan as they crossed the river and into their woods. In return I had many beautiful gifts from the children, all with elements of craft and nature. Archie made me an enormous card made out of felt with dried poppies glued on to it.

On our last visit to the woods, there was quite a crowd. Everyone came, including the newest families to join the group and some old attenders, Evan, Atticus and Jaime. We all squeezed into the dome. After the lunch Jenny G. presented me with a cake, which we carefully carved into thirteen pieces. She had also made a mobile with origami birds on which some people from the group had written messages. They indicated, above all else, how significant our mornings in this place had been for everyone who had participated. Jay wrote, "Remember this and you will have eternal happiness, 'Things come and things go.' "

I wondered about it all the way home. I wondered, and not for the first time, if I should be staying, if the group was enough to hold me here in Lincoln, a town that had initially been so far from the familiar. I wondered how it had crept up on me and become the familiar. I bemoaned the fact that we would no longer see the seasons change and change again in these woods: the cyclical secret missing from the end of Jay's wisdom, for things come and things go and things come back again. That is the seasons. But what of the children? They grow linearly, always leaving something behind,

The woods were still not only on us in smoke and moss and cake crumbs, but inside us, too.

always moving forward with a fascination in the present and themselves and a sense, albeit unconscious, of the moments they are shedding, forever lost behind them. And I wondered if what Jay really wanted to pass on to me was the message that we hold within ourselves everything that we need to experience and be in the world, and that we should be ready to let the rest fall away.

So I felt, as Joel and Cedar and I cycled away, that the woods were still not only on us in smoke and moss and cake crumbs, but inside us, too. Will Cedar remember the trees? Will Onyx remember singing the fire alight? Will Oscar remember making pancakes? Will Archie remember being a bee? At the smell of fallen leaves in the autumn will Elise remember burying herself in the pile around which we sang our songs? It hardly mattered. Heartwood had been planted in them as it had been planted in me.

Summer Poems, Songs, and Crafts

June, Lovely June
Traditional

June, love - ly June, that beau - ti - fies the ground, The
song___ of the cuck - oo in the green woods re - sound!

Busy Bee
Words and music by Candy Verney, from *The Singing Year* (Hawthorn Press, 2006).

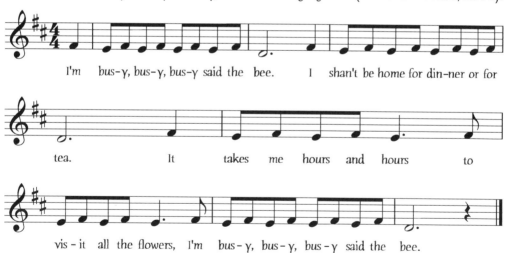

I'm bus-y, bus-y, bus-y said the bee. I shan't be home for din-ner or for
tea. It takes me hours and hours to
vis - it all the flowers, I'm bus-y, bus-y, bus-y said the bee.

Fire Child
Traditional Native American chant

Fire_child sing, fire_ child_dance! Fire child you are mine.

Fire_child sing, fire_ child_dance! Fire child you are mine. Light

stream - ing, light stream - ing. Watch-ing my fire child grow. Light

stream - ing, light stream - ing. Watch-ing my fire child grow.

Whitsun dove and wreath

1. Cut a dove shape out of thin white card. Cut a slit in the middle of the shape.

2. Cut a square of white tissue paper about 4 x 4 inches. Accordion-fold the tissue paper so that it will fit into the slit you have cut in the bird.

3. Insert the folded tissue paper into the slit in the bird so that there is equal tissue paper on either side of the bird's body.

4. Open out the accordion fold and glue together the pieces that meet at the top over the bird's body. Thread a needle with white thread and carefully sew on to the top of the tissue paper wings, leaving a long piece for connecting on to the wreath.

5. With willow or ivy make a secure circle. Decorate it with white or gold ribbons. From this simple wreath hang the doves at various heights.

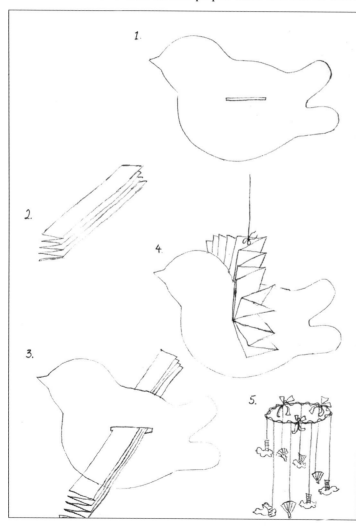

Felt Swan

(thanks to the lovely lady in the fairtrade yurt in Tserseleg, Mongolia)

What you will need:

- Strong white felt (wool felt is best)
- A small piece of black, orange, yellow felt for the beak
- White thread, black or brown thread and thread of a similar color as the felt for the beak
- Needle and pins
- Scissors
- Stuffing (carded wool top is best)

1. Use the pattern to cut out the correct number of pieces. Use black, orange or yellow felt for the beak and white felt for all other pieces.

2. With stitches sew the base on to one of the sides. (Pattern indicates where to do this.)

3. Sew the two sides together evenly and then sew the second side of the base on to the second side of the swan.

4. Leave two openings for stuffing, one in the breast of the bird, below the neck and one where the beak will go eventually.

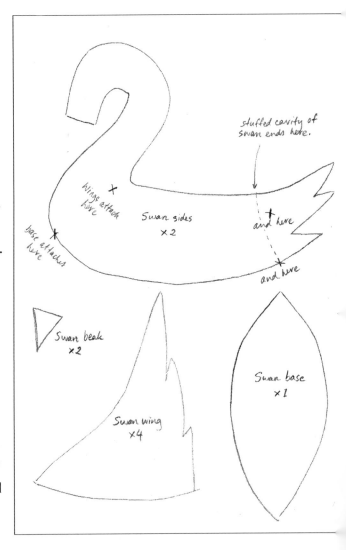

stuffed cavity of swan ends here.

wings attach here

Swan sides × 2

and here

base attaches here

and here

Swan beak × 2

Swan base × 1

Swan wing × 4

5. Sew the tail end of the swan closed in a straight line (indicated on pattern) from where the base attaches to the top of the swan. The two sides of the tail feathers are not sewn together but are kept separate.

6. Use the end of a pencil or a knitting needle to push wool stuffing into the swan, making sure that the neck and base of the neck in particular are tightly stuffed. There should be no floppiness to the neck.

7. Sew up the hole in the breast.

8. Sew each side of the beak on to the swan, closing the opening at the "nose" end of the swan.

9. Use dark thread to stitch two eyes onto either side of the swan's "face."

10. Sew two swan wings together and then another two. (This doubles up the thickness of the felt and allows the wings to stand proudly off the body of the swan.)

11. Sew the base of each wing onto the sides of the swan (as indicated on pattern).

Epilogue

*F*or my family there have been other woods and other playgroups in the great outdoors since our group in Heartwood. But none of them capture the significance of the community we created in the woods outside Lincoln. I have tried to make sense of its certain something, its spirit. Was its warmth inspired by the generosity with which Jane and Nick shared their private property? Was it the unique collection of individuals? Or the lack of other such activities on offer in the region? Was it to do with the stage of life my family and I were passing through at the time? I am sure all of the above and much more determined its importance to me.

We have kept in touch with the families that attended our group and once a year, in the summer, we have a reunion in Heartwood, camping amongst the trees. Some of us camp for a few nights, others just pass through for a visit, catching up on the year, seeing how each others' children have changed, meeting new babies. Fires are built, food is cooked, stories are told and as the children grow the games evolve and change. Dressing up and face-painting featured heavily this summer. Elise and Cedar began by being woodland princesses and fairies, casting spells with wands and painted nails. Then Onyx and Archie introduced some face paint, the colors were mixed and re-mixed and soon the dresses were replaced by blackened body paint. The children tore through the trees, part naked, smeared with color, growling and climbing! The wild woods had returned.

Left: Onyx, Archie and Jenny G. "cooking" leaves and sticks

About the Author

*M*argaret Loescher is a writer of fiction and non-fiction and a mother of two young daughters. Sometimes these roles support one another and often times they challenge one another. They both sustain her. She has worked as a Waldorf kindergarten assistant for a short time and now leads "Woodmice," an outdoor parent-and-child group in a local nature reserve. She is a Quaker and helps facilitate her local Children's Meeting. A storyteller at home, in schools, in Quaker Meeting, and in the woods, she lives with her husband and children in Cambridge, UK. She is represented by the Wylie Agency in New York.

53990899R00052

Made in the USA
Charleston, SC
23 March 2016